5—16—16

D1051002

Gifts with No Giver

Gifts with No Giver

a love affair with truth

Poems by Nirmala

Endless Satsang Foundation

Nirmala offers these poems in gratitude for the love and grace that flow through his teacher, Neelam, and in gratitude for the blessings of truth brought to this world by Ramana Maharshi and H.W.L. Poonja.

In addition he would like to thank Donald Turcotte for his generous assistance in the design and production of this collection, and also Pamela Wilson for her help with editing.

Copyright © 1999 by Daniel Erway (Nirmala)
First Edition: 1999
Second Edition: 2008

ISBN for this second edition: 978-1-4382-6917-7

Cover Photo: © Tihis www.dreamstime.com

Endless Satsang Foundation, Inc.
Nirmalanow@aol.ocm
www.endless-satsang.com

to Neelam
the blue sapphire flame in my heart

your hand is always in mine
your whispered endearments are my constant
    companion
you have never turned your face from me
no matter how many times I have turned from
    you

        now I vow undying love
        I meet you in the secret places I used to
           hide from you in
        I hold you with tenderness I used to
           reserve for my pain
        I would give you my life and my breath
        in
           an instant

for you are my true love
the one with no form
the one who has never been anywhere, but
    right here
in the singing of my heart

why fear this moment
when no thoughts come
at last I lie naked
in the arms of experience

why fear this moment
when no words come
at last I find rest
in the lap of silence

why fear this moment
when love finds itself alone
at last I am embraced
by infinity itself

why fear this moment
when judgment falls away
at last my defenses
fail to keep intimacy at bay

why fear this moment
when hope is lost
at last my foolish dreams
are surrendered to perfection

I may think I feel love
but it is love that feels me
constantly testing the woven fibers
that enclose and protect my heart
with a searing flame
that allows no illusion of separation

and as the insubstantial fabric of my inner
    fortress
is peeled away by the persistent fire
I desperately try to save some charred remains
by escaping into one more dream of passion
I may think I can find love
but it is love that finds me

meanwhile, love becomes patient and lies in
    wait
its undying embers gently glowing
and even if I now turn and grasp after the
    source of warmth
I end up cold and empty-handed
I may think I can possess love
but it is love that possesses me

and finally, I am consumed
for love has flared into an engulfing blaze
that takes everything
and gives nothing in return
I may think love destroys me
but it is love that sets me free

the past is long gone
from here
there is no way back
how could there be

      the present is over too quickly
      for feeble desires
      to have any effect
      except to hide peace

the future races ahead
forever out of reach
of dreamy wishes
and useless plans

      and yet when I rest
      in the endless now
      every need is satisfied
      in ways never imagined

I have fallen in love with truth
I only want to be with her
I cannot stand to be apart
I would gladly go to the ends of the earth
or I would never again move from this spot
just to be sure to inhale her fragrant perfume
with my dying breath

I have fallen in love with truth
her every wish my command
I simply must obey
for she has captured my soul
and taken complete control
of even my innermost thoughts
freeing me to find repose
in her unadorned splendor

I have fallen in love with truth
with exquisite tenderness she shows me
the perfection in my every flaw
no need for pretense
for she knows everything about me
and yet takes me in her arms
with complete abandon
until only she remains

sunlight burns
shadow cools
there is no difference

earth is still
grass is moving
there is no difference

wind rustles
sky is silent
there is no difference

spider drifts by on a silken web
and I remain
there is no difference

where is absence of desire
once I dreamed there would only be bliss
now I am in awe of the ordinary
now I am content with longing or no longing
desires do not disturb the source of all desire
life and death carry on as they always have
and always will

only the dreamer is gone

behind the flow of imagination
beyond any effort to be still
dancing in the ebb and flow of attention
more present than the breath
I find the origins of my illusions

only the dreamer is gone
        the dream never ends

river of voices
eternal mantra of foam
meaningless words swallowed in a humming
   roar
thoughts arise and are splashed away

     river of music
     sacred song of motion
     nowhere to go but downstream
     actions arise and are swept away

river of sounds
laughing and crying
impossible to bring the depths to the surface
emotions arise and are washed away

     river of silence
     flowing through everything
     peace beyond even the absence of sound
     nothing ever arises

I don't know what to say
I never know what to say
yet there is great power in not knowing
knowing I can never know
        the mystery constantly deepens
        overwhelming my sense of what is
        the mystery speaks without words
        taking the breath away
        leaving no air for words
in silence there is room for pain and bliss
in unlimited measure

love is a dream
that does not stop
when you awaken
but constantly surprises
no strong emotions
stirring up dust
and clouding your vision

      love is more than it seems
      and has a purpose
      you cannot see
      and yet cannot hide from

love is an inescapable reality
that knocks you senseless
takes your breath away
and leaves no heart beating
      but its own

nobody is my lover
       I searched for her for lifetimes
       and finally noticed
       she was always at my side
nothing is my heart's true desire
       but something
       used to always get in the way
now emptiness fills me to overflowing
as I fall into my lover's embrace
       I can love you or ...
       I can love love itself
       and thus love you truly
       letting illusion rest at last
has freedom spoiled me for any other lover
or is there room for the one in the infinite
questions fall away in the embrace of my true
   love
       join me in her arms
       and rest at last
I am carried
like a mother holding her infant child
tender, yet firm
       I am provided for
       with caring attention
       that anticipates every need
and yet
I am swallowed whole by this love

no longer my hand that moves
no longer my voice that muses
no longer my eyes that fill with tears
at the simple beauty of a hazy afternoon

who could contain this rapture
who keeps this heart beating
who could keep this heart from breaking
at the loss of everything it foolishly held dear

questions have lost their fascination
longing has surrendered to fullness
gratitude is enough
even with the loss of everything
      foolishly held dear

endless traces of memory
fill in empty moments
stealing my peace
and robbing my happiness
they cannot take the real treasure
beyond peace and happiness

behind every memory
is simple awareness
of this ordinary moment
a body breathing
a mind making comparisons
and yet something more
is always present

this simple moment
a body still breathing
mind still chasing dreams
what is the something more
that fills the ordinary with magic?
the full recognition
of what was always longed for
in the heart

through emptiness
peace is born
no painful labor required
an easy birth
an easy life
an easy death
the peace flows from the depths
the heart can only be broken
when the object of love is gone
but true love has no object
    through emptiness
    awareness is born
    it grows untended
    filling the emptiness with eyes
    and ears and noses
    and more hearts
    to be broken and mended
    broken and mended
    until they can no longer
    be broken
    only mended
through awareness
birth is ended
what never ends needs no beginning
love is too large
for a heart to hold
yet the opened heart
rests in this largeness
until fear is also ended
knowing the heart
has always been
unbroken

no poem
no song
no ritual
captures the simple beingness of a stone
        let alone a mountain of stone

but let the stone write the poem
let the mountain sing in your heart
let the rituals fall like gentle rain to nourish
the gods inside every stone
    and every mountain
let your soul rise above the mountain
        above the rain
        above the clouds
the journey home requires no effort
only willingness to release your claw like grip
    on the familiar ground

then the stone speaks unspeakable truth
then the mountain fills your heart with a silent
    song of peace
and rituals sprout wings of surrender in your
    soul
        and you arrive
                here

like a green desert
life has burst forth
in this empty container
spilling over
and moistening the parched soil

       no need to store the bounty
       the supply is endless
       the source is at hand
       the fruits of no labor
       within easy reach

feast on this
feed the deepest longing
drink until thirst is a distant memory
desire itself is consumed
when the heart finds nourishment

your smile
morning sun on new fallen snow
melting the icy chill
unveiling a blue sapphire flame in my heart
burning memory into ash
revealing bliss
       your eyes
       dark liquid pools of grace
       causing a whirlpool of emotion
       carrying me to the depths
       drowning me in joy
your touch
gentlest breeze
passing through skin and flesh and bone
healing so complete
leaving no scars
where once were deep wounds
       your form
       graceful flight in empty sky
       giving me birth
       naming me
       ruling me forever
       yet your only command: setting me free
your voice
birdsong and distant thunder
inspiring quiet so vast
thinking no longer finds refuge
       your love
       a rain swollen river
       overflowing its banks
       washing away all cherished possessions
       leaving an empty cup
       full of peace

I never knew tears could feel so good
until I opened my heart
and found they come from the same source
as boundless laughter

instead of blurring my vision
they bring beauty into focus

instead of burning my cheeks
they wash away dusty dryness I used to hide
   behind

let sorrow have me now
for surrender has freed me to savor
the bittersweet nectar
that flows in measureless abundance
        from within

I bathe in holy water
wash myself clean in the sacred river
nothing has changed
yet senses are now clear
and I hear what she is saying to my heart:

> give me your foolish thoughts...
>   you don't need them anymore
> give me your every desire...
>   they will never fulfill you
> give me your deepest fears...
>   what use have they ever been to you
> give me your very soul...
>   you have always been too large
>   for its tight confines

so once again I plunge into Ganga's embrace.

> once for my thoughts
> once more for my desires
> and a third time for my fears

she has always had my soul

and once again, nothing has changed....
>   nothing always changes

no deep rooted fears
fear exists on the surface
fear is the surface
dive deeper and fear is swallowed
in the depth of knowing

nothing to fear in this moment
even when a gun is held to your head
the thing most feared has not yet happened
once an event has occurred
fear is too late

fear has no home here
where all is as it is
Breathe the tranquil air
and discover the fragrant serenity

thoughts dance their enticing moves
before my entranced inner sight
but the spell is broken
when I wonder
who is entranced

      memories beckon seductively
      with all the luster they can
      manage
      yet their shine is swallowed
      in the light
      behind my eyes

there is one dancer
I cannot resist
her only movement is utter stillness
I find no memory
in her transparent gaze

romance is a simple mistake
finding true love
in the arms of one other
is like capturing a waterfall
in a tiny cup
thirst is slightly quenched
why not just step into the source

romance is a beautiful distraction
taking you beyond your dry concerns
yet what good is an open heart
with room for only one
when that one is gone
the heart is empty and dry
and tears fall on empty ground

romance is a single drop
in a torrent of love
why settle for one sip at a time
the sweetest tasting water is deeper than the
    surface
dive into the current
and as you are swept away
drink to your heart's content

nothing seen is wasted
the sight of every eye
increases the range of vision
of that which sees
 every sight is a gem
 of pure perfection
 in the inner eyes
 of that which sees
each viewpoint
lives on forever
nothing can die
within that which sees
 look deeply into any eye
 beyond your reflection
 come face to face
 with that which sees
abandon appearance
let go of pretense
you are naked and exposed
before that which sees
 do not turn away your gaze
 no need to hide
 only love shines in the eyes
 of that which sees

all may have a mind of their own
but thoughts are gifts of grace
touching mind for an instant
like melting snowflakes

      every place can be home
      but rest is a divine blessing
      when effort falls away
      like the setting sun

the heart may burn with emptiness
but love comes in waves
smoothing away doubts
like a tide erasing footprints in the sand

in the dream
I always play the fool
in the dream
my defenses always fail
in the dream
my desires are never fully satisfied
in the dream
my heart is broken over and over

    wide awake
    I always play the fool
    wide awake
    my defenses always fail
    wide awake
    my desires are never fully
    satisfied
    wide awake
    my heart sings its endless joy

what should we do
what is the purpose of life
here is the endless task
to do nothing well
here is your purpose
to be free of any purpose

why do we suffer so
how can we end the pain
here is the source of suffering
in the desire to end suffering
there is no end to pain
nor an end to joy
within the soul of freedom

my longing was never deep enough
to touch this empty well
    my effort was never great enough
    to move this unmovable mountain
my understanding was never broad enough
to contain this silent truth
    my dreaming was never real enough
    to shape this formless presence
        nothing is always enough
        when nothing is needed

the mystery
of this simple moment
cannot be spoken
yet all of history
occurred to arrive here
       the mystery
       of the endless terrain of self
       cannot be mapped out
       countless new frontiers
       are born with every breath
the mystery
of awakening
cannot be achieved
all that is needed
is to notice inner eyes that never close
       the mystery
       of sweet undying love
       cannot be understood
       the heart already knows
       what the mind can only long for
the mysteries
always remain
untouched by worried thought
ready to welcome us home
when we abandon our dreams

take my hand
feel the vital grip
that love lends to this flesh
     listen to my voice
     hear the catch in my throat
     of awe that can't be expressed
gaze into my eyes
see tears welling up
as I recognize my long lost self in your
smile
     rest in my arms
     find refuge in my embrace
     until you know you are forever
safe
join me now
here
where we have never parted

no word is real enough
to conjure up a crumb of bread
still we try to find nourishment
in endless musing

no thought is thick enough
to cushion a fall
yet we pursue idle distractions
while tripping on obstacles in our path

there is a silent voice behind the words
there is a quiet source of every thought
listen without your ears
ponder without your mind

      rest your senses and your sense
      for just one moment of this stillness
      will sustain and uphold you forever

it is here
in the breath
it is here
in the stillness between breaths
      it is here
      in the active mind
      it is here
      in the resting mind
it is here
in the dream's panorama
it is here
in each moment of awakening
      it is here
      when all is well
      it is here
      when fear has nothing left to fear
even then
there is pure noticing
even then
there is no need for doing
      no frantic searching
      can find the obvious
      no seeking needed
      to find that which seeks
it is here
where it can never be lost
or found

where does willingness come from
willing to do anything
      although nothing can be done
willing to surrender everything
      although nothing is mine
willing to be exposed
      although there is nothing to hide

where does lovingness come from
loving the flaws in us
      although we are perfect
loving the simplicity
      although feelings are so complex
loving you
      although no one is there

where does gratefulness come from
grateful for the laughter
      although the joke is on me
grateful for the beauty
      although eyes cannot truly see
grateful for the bounty
      although hands are forever empty

truth is a living being
that must be nourished and fed
and loved
then it grows and blossoms
filling the air with pure aroma
making us gasp with delight

truth is a friend
that asks for loyalty
and acceptance
then it enters our hearts
dissolving the boundaries
freeing us from loneliness

truth is a demanding lover
that requires constant affection
and endless gifts
then it rewards us
with a glimpse of indescribable beauty
making us faint with satisfaction

and finally truth is an empty hand
that asks for and requires
nothing

the obvious signs
a playful smile
absence of pretense
disregard for convention
respect for truth
      listen when they speak
      look where they point
      follow where they lead
abandon hope and faith and dreams
accept nothing less than all they have to give
      your share in the infinite is infinite
      come claim your birthright
return to the place never left
return and let the seeker rest
      subside in the unending peace
let the seeker rest
      let that which you seek find you
let the seeker rest
      the task is finished
          let the seeker rest
             let the seeker rest

behind closed eyes
the world falls away
a whirl of empty sensation
with no boundary
drowning thought
in a silent symphony
burning the body
in painless effigy
when eyes open again
the world is cleansed
only perfection remains
the room is resplendent
with the absence of illusion

grateful
for grace
that fills mind with visions
of the invisible

grateful
for time
that expands to embrace
stillness

grateful
for breath
that seems to require
no breather

grateful
for gratitude
that breaks the soul wide open
freeing love

in a timeless instant
before a painful idea appears in my mind
an ever present softness, a gentle hand
reaches into my thoughts
and soothes them
until they reflect only empty sky

> in a timeless moment
> before a desire burns in my heart
> an inexhaustible peace, a whispered
> silence
> quells the storm of fruitless wishing
> leaving me breathlessly still

in a timeless lifetime
before my story is wrenched from silence
a wordless honesty, an unflinching gaze
shows me my face
without shadows of doubt
dimming the fire within

> in a timeless eternity
> before my soul is torn from infinity
> a passionate tenderness, an enfolding
> embrace
> leaves me alone
> with the source of sweetness
> even closer than a kiss

welcome home
welcome to the home never left
you have always lived here
will always live here
      this is home, forever...
so stop now
no effort is required
even during all journeys
you have always been here
      this is home, forever...
so relax now
the fire is in the hearth
this inner fire is keeping you warm
the storms outside cannot touch you
      this is home, forever...
so rest now
everyone loved is right here
we have always lived here
will always live here
      this is home, forever...

I must follow this thought
     all the way
let the mind have its way with me
     but only with me
not with the quiet presence
     the voice behind all thoughts

I must feel this emotion
with my whole being
and as it sweeps me off my feet
enjoy the sensation of falling
falling endlessly into the arms
     of no lover

I must, I must
for this dream demands no less
than total suspension of disbelief
total surrender
for the dream and the dreamer
are one and the same

I have never been more than a dream
and the dreamer
is awake

endless poems wait to be written
        while all has been said before
        this truth cannot be spoken
and so I try again
just to get a little closer
to the unspeakable reality

forever gently teasing just out of reach
forever invisible at the edge of perception
forever tranquil in the maelstrom of feelings
forever present in this moment's eternity

it doesn't matter
what I do
mind judges
then judges itself for judging
that's just what minds do
when I let it have its way
it surprises me by stopping
and in the vacant interlude
the mind finds no grip
and falls effortlessly
into the deep pool of silence
it never left

rain falls
within the endless awareness
the sun still shines
behind the clouds

loss rips
at the heart of love
empty peace still rests
at the source of tears

floods wash
away the precious hillsides
life rises to the surface
for another breath of joy

thoughts race
across the mind's attention
quiet still sings
from the throat of nowhere

pure freedom remains
when all else is
      swallowed in the river of time

mind always wins
every thought an artful trap
leading further into dreams
resistance speeds the entanglement
surrender, the only option

    then what surprising silence
    entanglement becomes a tender caress
    dreaming dissolves in wonder

mind continues the endless game
jumping in to claim peace as its own
creating a new identity to play with
as if it could find something solid in empty
   space
laughter, the only response

    then identities come and go
    mind plays on the surface
    silence enjoys it all

all I have ever wanted is wanting
all I have ever had is having
all I am is all there is
and wanting and having are always here
        in equal measure

all I have ever loved is love
all I have ever loved is loving
all I am is love
and loving is always here
        in infinite measure

quite ordinary desires
come and go
come and go
never needing to be fulfilled
their satisfaction made irrelevant
by the shining beauty
        of a rain soaked forest
the rain washing away thoughts
        of something lacking

what could be lacking
in this explosion of life
that grows in each nook and cranny
        of the infinite heart
the moisture of love
seeping down to nourish the roots
        of every being
or dancing in streams and rivers
        all the way home

die a little
with every disappointment
or find what never dies
and has no preferences

try a little
and keep illusion going
or see the futility of effort
and stop pushing on nothing

be happy a little
now and then when circumstance allows
or rest in the source of happiness
now, then and always

believe a little
that you are someone
or notice there is no separate one
nor any limit to being

love a little
with half a heart
or let love have it all
filling the heart to overflowing

the dance of emptiness
goes on and on
colors, shapes and forms
arrayed in courtly splendor
on the dance floor of infinity

the patterns of the dance
will hypnotize if watched too closely
while the entire view
ends all trances
and frees the dreaming mind

now join the dance
its irresistible ebb and flow
swallows your pride
in the pure joy
of moving stillness

this voice is inadequate
to express the abundant wonder
of this endless moment

this body is insufficient
to embrace the sweet infinity
of this lover's bodiless form

these eyes are unable
to capture the invisible beauty
of a cloudless sky

and yet I sing with joy,
caress the air with tenderness,
allow beauty to fill my eyes with tears,
and know that the love in my heart
is always enough

truth is too simple for words
before thought gets tangled up in
nouns and verbs
there is a wordless sound
a deep breathless sigh
of overwhelming relief
to find the end of fiction
in this ordinary
yet extraordinary moment
when words are recognized
      as words
and truth is recognized
      as everything else

a quiet room
empty of profound thoughts
in this moment
no need to uncover deep truths

the chairs do not mind the silence
the rug is not burdened by the lack of
    weighty ideas
only the thought, "there must be something
    more"
cries out in pretended anguish

the chairs pay no attention
the rug only lies more quietly
until the pretended suffering
can't help but notice
there is always more
        that does not need to be revealed

laughter stops thought
and fills the space behind the eyes with light
such simple delight
to find nothing is knowable

    I can only give everything
    to this nothing
    and am overjoyed
    to let it tear down the barricade in my
      chest
        and steal my heart

the room is empty
except for these saddened eyes
that find refuge in emptiness

    friends come and go
    lovers come and go
    but love itself never wavers

emptiness is my refuge
emptiness is my resting place
everywhere I turn, the end of boundaries
awaits

    take sadness now
    take happiness also
    leave only clear vision

the room is still empty
except for these opened eyes
that find refuge in fullness

early in the morning
asleep in a dream
only to awaken in another dream
why disturb the quiet mist
with imaginary forms
the heart is never fulfilled
with dream lovers

      for there is never enough
      of what does not satisfy

so let the mist have it all
I have moistened my cheeks long enough in
this fog of dreaming
I will not move again until my true love
appears

      when at last the sun burns away the
        haze
      no one is there
      what relief. . . to find her waiting

mind finds a path
to struggle along
never reaching the goal
heart knows it already rests
in the path of something wonderful
it cannot escape

       mind seeks to hold onto
       a still point
       of final understanding
       heart knows it is being held
       by an unmoving whirlwind
       that it will never comprehend

mind tries to feel safe enough
to allow love
out into the open
heart knows love is never cautious
and cannot be kept secret
once all hope of refuge is abandoned

simply resting
from a full day of resting
feeling too rested
to even consider anything more

simply quiet
staying in the silent pauses
no thought
not even the idea: no thought

too busy
doing nothing
to stop long enough
to do something less

excitement stirs the blood
yet only nothingness is ever palpable
imagined pleasures always fall short
  compared to the simple reality
    this bird in the hand
     is worth a million in the bush
sensations have their say
promising satisfaction, as if they could stay
  long enough to fulfill endless desire
  yet always ending in a reverberating
   empty stillness
this deafening calm
is cherished by the core of being
as the true source of infinity

light through a prism...
      a rainbow
love through my heart...
         the spectrum of feelings revealed
            red anger to blue sadness
            yellow fear to black despair
allow them back into my heart
and the prism works in reverse
turning the most deeply tinted pain
back into pure white love

foolish to chase after imaginary pleasures
they love to dance out of reach
giving only tastes of slight satisfaction

simpler to give heartfelt attention
to the source of contentment
and find there is never anything missing
        in this moment

then the rising water of devotion
takes the weight out of these hands
and dissolves the dreamlike boundaries
        of desire itself

a world of endless contradiction
sad smiles and joyous tears
the heart is torn in two
by feelings that never fail to pull in opposite
    directions
torn in two
by dreams that forever dance out of reach

until at last the contents of the heart
spill out in an endless flood
of sad smiles and joyous tears
that no longer have any ambivalence
because of their shared source

words do not come
there is no need for profound utterances or
   deep truths
here is an ordinary evening
why spoil it with dramatic overstatement

the silence amidst the noise
the gem at the core of every experience
is polished by simple attention
into shining magnificence

every taste
every sensation
every possible pleasure
is already present
in the timeless
awareness
that is beating my heart
what use
in chasing dreams
that have already
come true

who would have guessed
this empty feeling in my chest
is the door to eternity

who could have known
this longing
is what I longed for

how is it possible
thoughts of freedom
only hide freedom

why don't I care
about answers
when questions never end

who would have guessed
this empty feeling in my chest
could be so full

what kind of fire
has no preference for fuel
gladly burning thoughts, feelings,
    bodies and souls
yet it is a cool flame
leaving the core untouched

it flares whenever I give it attention
or has it always been burning this brightly

sleep comes in the afternoon
and then wakefulness never truly returns
drinking in rest like cool water
cold outside does not touch it
yawning does not disturb it
thoughts of friends in pain
can only make it more obvious
here in this quiet house
the totality comes out to play

hot sun fills the eyes to overflowing
while a cooling breeze of freedom lifts sweat
   from the brow
every experience from the past that visits now
is recognized for what it has always been
pure food for the dreaming oneness
the banquet continues with each breath

I feast now even on heartbreak and loss
as they burst the limits I held so dear
freeing me from resisting appetite
for fear of a taste of sour fruit

I also welcome the sweet dessert
   of quiet moments
truth with no trimmings
a simple meal of limitless portion
         every tender morsel of silence
         more filling than the last

desire
pure unadulterated longing
tears at the chest with such force
it seems the soul might leave
   just to find relief

sadness
bittersweet taste of emptiness
weighs on the shoulders
like a burden
   too heavy to bear

surrender
swallowing all pride
collapsing from all effort
only to find rest again
   in the depths of pain itself

why was I running from this profound
   silent joy

sweeter than any kiss
the taste of eternity
lingers on my lips
tasting me

only the slightest pause
before her passion
overwhelms my feigned resistance
and takes everything I have to give

if this lover breaks my heart
there will be no pieces left

gratitude burns in the chest
glad tears run down the cheeks
strange illusion fills the eyes
the hum of life thrills the ears
      no more sense of mine to senses
      the body no longer belongs to anyone
      leaving no one in the way
      of all a body can contain
      and all a body cannot touch

wonder awes the mind
inspiration raises the spirit
silence soothes the doubts
intuition speaks to the soul
      no more idea of someone with ideas
      knowing needs no knower
      freeing truth to expand
      into all mind can contain
      and all mind cannot even imagine

when I am held in your arms
even pain is pure bliss
dark thoughts of separation and lack
   are waves of pure pleasure
unfulfilled desire is complete ecstasy

thank you
for never having let go

the truth catches up with me
I am not enough
never have been
never will be
what relief to admit this finite container
can never contain infinity
what joy to find infinity
needs no container

the tears flow freely now
the mind quiets and the heart breaks wide
   open
all the hopes and dreams of a lifetime, many
   lifetimes
gently washed away

      longings that have burned in the mind
         for ages
      suddenly flare up, but are quenched
      the dying embers of illusion
      gently washed away

and the soul thus unburdened of pretense
can barely stand to open its watery eyes
sights so intense, and yet so unreal
gently washed away

      finally, a voice that speaks the simplest
         of truth
      intermingled with sweet blissful sighs
      all the remaining fears and excitements
      gently laughed away

the tired wanderer
loses the strength to go on
and in surrendering to hopelessness
is surprised
to finally feel at home
      the hurried creek
      pauses in a cold, stony pool
      and in sudden stillness
      arrives at the distant ocean
the frightened warrior
decides, "I am ready to die"
and in willing abandon
becomes immortal
      the fitful breeze
      fades to calm in the afternoon heat
      and in catching its breath
      is reborn as undying tradewinds
the troubled philosopher
finds nothing to believe in
and in unexpected silence
just smiles
at the still unanswered questions
      the restless sea
      becomes smooth and mirrors the clouds
      and in ceasing all motion
      rejoins ts own depths
the saddened lover
faces the loss of illusion once again
and in dying to passion
falls in love
with love itself
      the weary sun
      sinks into the embrace of the horizon
      and in resting at last
      welcomes other shores to a new day

memories of true love
are useless in filling empty moments
for this lover never shows the same face
always a new disguise
keeping mind in suspense
and senses alert

surrender to perpetual surprise
and find her waiting once again
in emptiness itself

body is pure doing
        beyond doing there is mind
mind is pure knowing
        beyond knowing there is heart
                heart is pure being

mind is more than the brain
        the heart of being is infinitely more
        than this physical beating in the chest
all resides in this heart
the pulse of all life depends on its endless
rhythm
lifting us in moments of simple awareness
beyond the limits of doing and knowing
directly to the source
of our most tender feelings
        and beyond even limitless love
        where all is merged
                in silent wonder

the passion for freedom
swallows the source of passion
if twoness could lead to oneness
we would all be faithful lovers

no reason to dream of love
for it is already here in the waking heart
find it now
in the sweet infinity
of this moment's
eternal embrace

the flower can only wait
   for the bee to arrive
yet passion appears from nowhere
   to play hide and seek with peace
all that is gained is lost once again

timeless dreams are swallowed
   in the yawn of an awakened sleeper
yet spring rises like a phoenix
   from the ashes of winter
all that is lost was never real

is the heart big enough
for the source of weeping
is the heart big enough
for this pure delight

mind plays its oldest trick
sighing woe is me
so lonely
so lonely....being someone

what's this
a sweetness
in the embrace of loneliness
what deeper longing is being satisfied

I always thought you would come to me
      in the shape of a beautiful lover
I never dreamed you would steal my heart
      with no shape at all

I always pretended I needed arms to hold me
      and lips to kiss away my pain
yet I find fulfillment
      in the embrace of empty space

I always wished you would speak to me
      with words of tender sweetness
now I know you whisper silently
      of your undying love

I always knew I would find you
      although I foolishly looked with my eyes
you were here all along
      hiding just out of sight in my heart

a lasting marriage
when devotion has claimed you for its own
no longer any chance to stray
a brief fling with illusion no longer satisfies
the truth demands utter fidelity
with no possibility of divorce

all pain must be faced
and embraced as the true countenance of
    your beloved

all fear must be met
and recognized as the thrill of tasting
    the unknowable

all joy must be surrendered
and acknowledged as a gift with no giver

this union only requires telling the truth
even when the truth shatters your dreams
even when the truth leaves you emptied out
even when the truth reveals your counterfeit
    existence
then there is no other possibility
        than happily ever after

fire may burn the wood
the ashes do not mind

About the Author

After a lifetime of spiritual seeking, Nirmala met his teacher, Neelam, a devotee of H.W.L. Poonja (Papaji). She convinced Nirmala that seeking wasn't necessary; and after experiencing a profound spiritual awakening in India in 1998, he began offering satsang with Neelam's blessing. This tradition of spiritual wisdom has been most profoundly disseminated by Ramana Maharshi, a revered Indian saint, who was Papaji's teacher. Nirmala's perspective was also greatly expanded by his friend and teacher, Adyashanti.

Nirmala is also the author of *Nothing Personal, Seeing Beyond the Illusion of a Separate Self* and other writings that are available as free downloads on his website at **www.endless-satsang.com**. In addition to giving satsang throughout the U.S. and Canada, Nirmala is available for Nondual Spiritual Mentoring sessions in person or over the phone (see below). Nirmala lives in Sedona, Arizona with his wife, Gina Lake. More info about Gina and her books, including *Radical Happiness: A Guide to Awakening,* is at: www.radicalhappiness.com.

About Nondual Spiritual Mentoring

Nondual Spiritual Mentoring is available to support you in giving attention to the more subtle and yet more satisfying inner dimensions of your being. Whether for a single spiritual mentoring session or for ongoing one-to-one spiritual guidance, it is an opportunity for you to more completely orient your life towards the true source of peace, joy, and happiness. Nirmala has worked with thousands of individuals and groups around the world to bring people into a direct experience of the spiritual truth of oneness beyond the illusion of separation. Mentoring sessions are offered in person or over the phone and typically last an hour. To arrange an appointment, please email Nirmala at nirmalanow@aol.com.

10361424R0

Made in the USA
Lexington, KY
17 July 2011